D1261926

COUNTRY PROFILES

CHILE

BY CHRIS BOWMAN

BELLWETHER MEDIA • MINNEAPOLIS, MN

Blastoff! Discovery launches a new mission: reading to learn. Filled with facts and features, each book offers you an exciting new world to explore!

This edition first published in 2020 by Bellwether Media, Inc.

No part of this publication may be reproduced in whole or in part without written permission of the publisher.
For information regarding permission, write to Bellwether Media, Inc., Attention: Permissions Department,
6012 Blue Circle Drive, Minnetonka, MN 55343.

Library of Congress Cataloging-in-Publication Data

Names: Bowman, Chris, 1990- author.
Title: Chile / by Chris Bowman.
Description: Minneapolis, MN : Bellwether Media, Inc., 2020. | Series: Blastoff! discovery: country profiles | Includes bibliographical references and index. | Audience: Ages: 7-13 | Audience: Grades: 4-6 | Summary: "Engaging images accompany information about Chile. The combination of high-interest subject matter and narrative text is intended for students in grades 3 through 8"– Provided by publisher.
Identifiers: LCCN 2019034871 (print) | LCCN 2019034872 (ebook) | ISBN 9781644871676 (library binding) | ISBN 9781618918437 (ebook)
Subjects: LCSH: Chile–Juvenile literature. | Chile–Social life and customs–Juvenile literature.
Classification: LCC F3058.5 .B67 2020 (print) | LCC F3058.5 (ebook) | DDC 983–dc23
LC record available at https://lccn.loc.gov/2019034871
LC ebook record available at https://lccn.loc.gov/2019034872

Editor: Rebecca Sabelko   Designer: Brittany McIntosh

Printed in the United States of America, North Mankato, MN.

TABLE OF CONTENTS

THE STATUES OF EASTER ISLAND

MOAI STATUES AT TONGARIKI

A family takes a trip to the remote Easter Island. First, they go for a hike around the Rano Raraku **volcano**. Hundreds of towering human-head statues, called *moai*, stand looking upon the island. On average, they are about 13 feet (4 meters) tall! Their defined brows and noses give each statue a similar look. These ancient figures were likely built to honor important **ancestors** and chiefs.

MANY NAMES

In Spanish, Easter Island is known as *Isla de Pascua*. Native peoples of the island call it *Rapa Nui*, meaning "Great Rapa," and *Te Pito te Henua*, "Navel of the World."

OTHER TOP SITES

LAUCA NATIONAL PARK

SAN CRISTOBAL HILL

SAN RAFAEL GLACIER

TORRES DEL PAINE NATIONAL PARK

Then the family stops by Tongariki. They admire the 15 moai standing in a row. That afternoon, the family relaxes on the white-sand Anakena Beach. The history and the beaches of Easter Island are just some of the things that Chile has to offer!

Chile is a long, narrow country on the southwestern coast of South America. It spans 291,933 square miles (756,102 square kilometers). Santiago, the capital city, rests near the center of the country. The city is surrounded by the Andes Mountains.

EASTER ISLAND

The western shores of Chile face the Pacific Ocean. Peru and Bolivia border Chile to the north, while Argentina lies to the east. Chile's southern tip is called *Tierra del Fuego*, which means "land of fire." It is separated from the rest of the country by the **Strait** of Magellan.

PACIFIC OCEAN

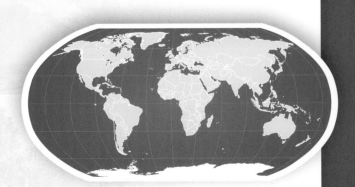

PERU

BOLIVIA

ANTOFAGASTA

VALPARAÍSO

ARGENTINA

CONCEPCIÓN

SANTIAGO

CHILE

THE SKINNY

On average, Chile is about 110 miles (177 kilometers) across. Its length is more than 20 times its width!

STRAIT OF MAGELLAN

TIERRA DEL FUEGO

LANDSCAPE AND CLIMATE

Chile's long shape includes many different landscapes. Much of the north is covered by the dry Atacama Desert. This area is among the driest in the world! The steep slopes of the Andes Mountains run the length of Chile's eastern border. A long valley with **fertile** soil lines the Andes' western edge. Rounded mountains run along the Pacific coast.

= ATACAMA DESERT
= ANDES MOUNTAINS
= PATAGONIA

N
W + E
S

ATACAMA DESERT

HOT SPOT

The Chilean Andes are home to many active volcanoes. They are some of the highest points in the country. The tallest, Ojos del Salado, is 22,614 feet (6,893 meters) tall!

ANDES MOUNTAINS

SANTIAGO

Average seasonal highs and lows

JANUARY
HIGH: 84 °F (29 °C)
LOW: 54 °F (12 °C)

APRIL
HIGH: 73 °F (23 °C)
LOW: 45 °F (7 °C)

JULY
HIGH: 57 °F (14 °C)
LOW: 37 °F (3 °C)

OCTOBER
HIGH: 72 °F (22 °C)
LOW: 45 °F (7 °C)

°F = degrees Fahrenheit
°C = degrees Celsius

Central Chile is home to thick forests. Lakes and **glaciers** cover Patagonia in the south. Much of Chile has a **temperate** climate. Summers are often dry, and winters can be rainy. Patagonia is often cold and windy.

Chile can be a harsh place to live, but many animals still thrive! Llama-like guanacos roam from the northern Atacama Desert to southern Patagonia. Parrots and flamingoes fly over northern and central parts of the country.

Chinchillas hide high in the Andes while deer, such as huemuls, roam the rocky slopes. Pudu and monitos del monte live in Chile's forests. Raptors, such as the caracara, search Patagonia for prey. Off the nation's coasts, sea lions, dolphins, and whales break through the ocean's waves.

CHINCHILLA

PUDU

DARWIN'S FROG

MASTERS OF DISGUISE

Darwin's frogs were first noted by Charles Darwin in 1834. These frogs have a pointed nose and are shaped like a leaf. They live in southern Chile.

SOUTHERN CRESTED CARACARA

PATAGONIAN
HUEMUL

PATAGONIAN
HUEMUL

Life Span: **up to 14 years**
Red List Status: **endangered**

Patagonian huemul range =

LEAST CONCERN	NEAR THREATENED	VULNERABLE	ENDANGERED	CRITICALLY ENDANGERED	EXTINCT IN THE WILD	EXTINCT

Many of Chile's nearly 18 million people live near the middle of the country. Most Chileans are *mestizos* who have European and **native** backgrounds. Many are **descendants** of Araucanian (Mapuche), Aymara, and other native peoples.

The majority of Chileans belong to the Roman Catholic Church. This religion has given the country a strong feeling of **cultural** identity. There are also smaller communities of Protestants and Jehovah's Witnesses. Spanish is the national language of Chile. Some native communities speak their own languages as well.

FAMOUS FACE

Name: **Nicolás Massú**
Birthday: **October 10, 1979**
Hometown: **Viña del Mar, Chile**
Famous for: **A former professional tennis player who won two gold medals at the 2004 Olympic Games in Athens, Greece**

SPEAK SPANISH

SANTIAGO

ENGLISH	SPANISH	HOW TO SAY IT
hello	hola	OH-lah
goodbye	adiós	ah-dee-OHS
please	por favor	pohr fah-VOR
thank you	gracias	grah-SEE-ahs
yes	sí	SEE
no	no	noh

Most Chileans live in big cities, and many people have been moving to Santiago in recent years. They often rent apartments or live in single-family homes. Some people live in shantytowns called *callampas*. Chilean cities are known for their large **plazas**.

PLAZA DE ARMAS
CASTRO

Some **rural** Chileans own their own small farms, while others work on large estates. Highways and railroads connect these people to cities. Cars and buses are common all over Chile, but people in cities also take the subway and ride bicycles. In the south, Chileans often use ships to get around.

HUASOS WEARING CHAMANTOS

Rodeos are popular in southern parts of Chile. At these events, two cowboys, or *huasos*, ride horses while trying to trap a cow against a padded wall. They score points based on how well they pin the cow. Huasos wear straw hats and *chamantos*, or wool blankets with an opening for the head.

At planned events, it is not unusual for guests to arrive more than 30 minutes late. Hosts usually offer food and drinks at these gatherings. People often meet in the evening for *once*. They drink tea or coffee with light food. Chileans catch up with friends and family and talk about their days.

SIGN OF RESPECT

Chileans often use titles when they speak to others. It is common to address a man as *señor* and a woman as *señora* or *señorita*.

Chilean children must attend eight years of primary school. It is free through public schools. Secondary school lasts for four years. It includes two years of general education. Then students complete two years of more focused education. Chile is also known for its excellent colleges and universities.

More than two out of every three Chileans have **service jobs.** They work in **tourism** or in the government. Copper mining is also an important job in Chile. Chilean farmers grow many crops, such as grapes, avocados, and kiwis. In factories, workers make clothing, drinks, and machinery.

FACTORY WORKER

FARMER

SOCCER

FIELD HOCKEY

Many native Chileans play an ancient game called *chueca*. In this game, players from each team use wooden sticks to try to hit a ball across the other team's goal line.

Chileans love to watch and play soccer. Fans cheer for the national team and the many Chilean club teams. Tennis, basketball, and horse racing also draw big crowds. In the mountains, downhill skiing is a favorite sport.

SKIING

On the coasts, Chileans enjoy spending the day at the beach. Fishing and boating are popular on Chile's lakes. Patagonia is famous for its hiking trails. In the cities, concerts and plays are favorite ways to enjoy the evening.

BOATING

CORRE, CORRE LA GUARACA

What You Need:
- 5 or more players
- a handkerchief
- an open space

How to Play:
1. All players except one sit in a circle. The remaining player runs around the circle with a handkerchief.
2. The players in the circle are not supposed to watch the runner. Instead, they sing: "Corre, corre, la Guaraca who looks back will be bopped on his head!"
3. The runner gently drops the handkerchief on a player's back. The runner then tries to make it around the circle before the other player notices.
4. If the player does not notice, then they are out.
5. If the player does notice, they must try to tag the runner before they make it around the circle.
6. If the runner is tagged, they are out. If the runner is not tagged, then the runner sits and the second player becomes the runner.

Chileans eat a lot of **hearty** foods like beans, corn, and potatoes. *Pastel de choclo* is a favorite casserole with corn and meat. *Empanadas*, or pastries with meats and vegetables, are also popular. Near the coasts, Chileans enjoy seafood such as fish, squid, and shellfish.

Coffee and tea are popular drinks in Chile. *Agüita* is a favorite herbal tea. *Mote con huesillos* is a syrupy street drink. It combines peaches, wheat, sugar, and cinnamon for a refreshing treat on warm days.

PASTEL DE CHOCLO

MOTE CON HUESILLOS

COMPLETO

Have an adult help you make this easy and fun Chilean recipe!

Ingredients:

4 hot dogs and buns
1 avocado, halved and pitted
1 lime, cut into wedges
1 teaspoon minced garlic
1/2 cup sauerkraut
1/4 cup mayonnaise
2 teaspoons hot sauce
1/2 teaspoon lime juice
1/4 teaspoon salt

Steps:

1. Cook the hot dogs per the instructions on the package.

2. Mash the avocado until smooth. Stir in the hot sauce, garlic, lime juice, and salt.

3. Set hot dogs in buns, and add 3 tablespoons of the avocado mix, 2 tablespoons of sauerkraut, and 1 tablespoon of mayonnaise to each hot dog.

4. Serve with lime wedges and enjoy!

MOVING AROUND

During the holiday of *La Minga* in Chiloé, communities come together to help their neighbors move houses or churches from one place to another. They often do this to find new farmland or if water levels rise.

24

Chileans honor **traditions** during their holidays. Music fills the air and thousands of dancers travel to La Tirana in northern Chile for the *Fiesta de La Tirana*. This three-day carnival in July celebrates the **patron saint** *Virgen del Carmen*. On September 18, many people spend Independence Day with friends and family at parks.

At the beginning of November, people sometimes travel great distances to be with family on All Saints' Day. Chileans remember their loved ones by visiting cemeteries and decorating graves with flowers. Christmas comes during summertime in Chile. Families celebrate with *asados*, or barbecues. Great food brings everyone together!

ALL SAINTS' DAY

1541
Santiago is formed as a Spanish settlement

1818
Chile becomes free from Spain

1970
Salvador Allende Gossens changes the government to a system of democratic socialism, where the leader is elected and business is owned by everyone

1884
Chile grows by one-third after defeating Peru and Bolivia in the War of the Pacific

1973
General Augusto Pinochet takes power as a harsh dictator after armed forces overthrow the government

1990
General Pinochet steps down as head of state

2008
The Chaiten volcano erupts
after 9,000 years of no activity

2010
A group of
33 miners are
saved after
being trapped
underground
for 69 days

2006
Michelle Bachelet
becomes Chile's first
female president

2010
A powerful earthquake
causes widespread
damage throughout
central Chile

Official Name: Republic of Chile

Flag of Chile: The Chilean flag has two horizontal bands, with a short white band on top and a full red band on the bottom. In the upper left corner is a blue square with a white star. Blue represents the sky, white is for the snow in the Andes, and red stands for independence.

Area: 291,933 square miles
(756,102 square kilometers)

Capital City: Santiago

Important Cities: Concepción, Valparaíso, Antofagasta, Viña del Mar

Population:
17,925,262 (July 2018)

WHERE PEOPLE LIVE

COUNTRYSIDE
12.4%

CITY
87.6%

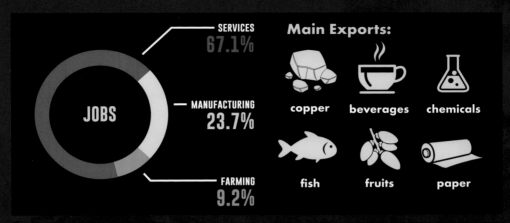

JOBS

SERVICES **67.1%**

MANUFACTURING **23.7%**

FARMING **9.2%**

Main Exports:

copper   beverages   chemicals

fish   fruits   paper

National Holiday:
Independence Day (September 18)

Main Language:
Spanish

Form of Government:
presidential republic

Title for Country Leader:
president

RELIGION

PROTESTANT **16.4%**

OTHER **5.4%**

NONE **11.5%**

ROMAN CATHOLIC **66.7%**

Unit of Money:
Chilean peso

GLOSSARY

ancestors—relatives who lived long ago

cultural—relating to the beliefs, arts, and ways of life in a place or society

descendants—people related to a person or group of people who lived at an earlier time

fertile—able to support growth

glaciers—massive sheets of ice that cover large areas of land

hearty—plentiful and satisfying

native—originally from the area or related to a group of people that began in the area

patron saint—a saint who is believed to look after a country or group of people

plazas—public squares in a city or town

rural—related to the countryside

service jobs—jobs that perform tasks for people or businesses

strait—a narrow channel connecting two large bodies of water

temperate—associated with a mild climate that does not have extreme heat or cold

tourism—the business of people traveling to visit other places

traditions—customs, ideas, or beliefs handed down from one generation to the next

volcano—a hole in the earth; when a volcano erupts, hot ash, gas, or melted rock called lava shoots out.

TO LEARN MORE

AT THE LIBRARY

Burgan, Michael. *Chile.* New York, N.Y.: Children's Press, 2017.

Leaf, Christina. *Argentina.* Minneapolis, Minn.: Bellwether Media, 2020.

Stine, Megan. *Where Is Easter Island?* New York, N.Y.: Penguin Workshop, 2017.

ON THE WEB

FACTSURFER

Factsurfer.com gives you a safe, fun way to find more information.

1. Go to www.factsurfer.com.

2. Enter "Chile" into the search box and click 🔍.

3. Select your book cover to see a list of related web sites.

INDEX

The images in this book are reproduced through the courtesy of: emperorcosar, front cover, p. 5 (Torres del Paine National Park); Daboost, pp. 4-5; Nick.bailey360, p. 5 (Lauca National Park); Mizzick, p. 5 (San Cristobal Hill); ajiber, p. 5 (San Rafael Glacier); Skreidzeleu, p. 8; Marianna Ianovksa, p. 9 (top); kavram, p. 9 (bottom); TheRocky41, p. 10 (caracara); Kuznetsov Alexey, p. 10 (chinchilla); poeticpenguin, p. 10 (pudu); Nature Picture Library / Alamy Stock Photo, p. 10 (frog), pp. 10-11; Anton_Ivanov, p. 12; Amp, p. 13 (top); wastesoul, p. 13 (bottom); Diego Grandi, p. 14; South America / Alamy Stock Photo, p. 15; Hemis / Alamy Stock Photo, p. 16; mauritius images GmbH / Alamy Stock Photo, p. 17; imageBROKER / Alamy Stock Photo, p. 18; Felipe Dipouy, p. 19 (top); Edwin Remsberg / Alamy Stock Photo, p. 19 (bottom); Lee Foster / Alamy Stock Photo p. 20 (top); dpa picture alliance / Alamy Stock Photo p. 20 (bottom); Agustina Camilion, p. 21 (top); ideabug, p. 21 (bottom); J. Enrique Molina / Alamy Stock Photo, p. 22; Larisa Blinova, p. 23 (middle), p. 23 (bottom); Tituz, pp. 24-25; FELIPE TRUEBA/EFE/Newscom, p. 25; Pictorial Press Ltd / Alamy Stock Photo, p. 26; diesgomo, p. 27 (top); Gobierno de Chile / Alamy Stock Photo, p. 27 (bottom); Glyn Thomas / Alamy Stock Photo, p 27 (paper); Fat Jackey p. 28 (coin).